Bischero
Book 1
Bee ska row

Introducing a travel adventure for the family.

By Janet Grace Milone
Illustrated by Ashton Riley
Edited by Josette Maltese-Perrie

First book of its kind!

Experience the Renaissance through the eyes of a druid child. His only way home is with the help of Time and Leonardo da Vinci. Experience his adventures city by city.

A new genre in Children's literature:

- ❖ The first book in a series of children's books for the traveler.
- ❖ A book that can be read by either child or parent, or both together.
- ❖ A book that is informative, entertaining, and educational.

3·30·15

To my dear cousins Anna and Carmellino,
May your ~~futt~~ lives be filled with
love and laughter always.
Love Janet Milone
OXOX

Vista Italia

First Edition March 2015

Copyright © 2003 Janet Grace Milone
All rights reserved

ISBN 978-0-9820672-0-8

Printed in the United States of America

To my sons, Joshua and Zachari, thank you for always igniting my spirit, and making my world sparkle. I love you!

Thank you my dear cousins, Nancie Buonomo Cenal and Josette Maltese-Perrie, for all of your support, and believing in me. I never would have been able to see my dream come to fruition without you at my side.

Acknowledgments

Several years ago, I had the privilege of meeting, and spending the day with **Alberto Ghiorso** (July 15, 1915 – December 26, 2010). A renowned nuclear scientist, from the University of California, Berkeley. I joined him on the Berkeley campus, and he was very proud to show me around his laboratory. On his office wall hung his certificate from the Guinness Book of World Records for creating the most elements on the periodic table: 12 chemical elements for which he had discovered or co-discovered.

Alberto had read "Bischero in Florence" prior to my arrival. He was very supportive of my work, and he shared his thoughts on alchemy. He explained to me how his colleagues had changed lead into gold by bombarding it with a tremendous amount of atomic particles, but it was costly, and only a small amount could be made. In short, it wasn't worth the effort. At 91yrs. old he was mentally sharp, and feisty over world events. In his newly acquired Toyota Prius, he drove us to his home where he cooked lunch. I will always be grateful to him for his kindness, and sharing his knowledge with me. We lost a treasure.

Did You Know...

"David"
By **Michelangelo**
He was 26yrs. old when
he carved the statue.

He created "David" from a block of Carrera marble that was in the trash pile. Michelangelo saw the image captured inside the stone and carved away with chisel and hammer to set it free.

Dominican Friars
Named after Saint
Dominic
Established in 1214

They had to take a vow of poverty. Known as the **Black Priests** because of their clothes. These were head of the inquisition and burned people at the stake for heresy.

Ghiberti, Lorenzo
1378-1455
Lived 77yrs

He created the golden doors for the baptistery of St. John. When **Michelangelo** saw them, he was so overcome by their beauty that he called them the **Gates of Paradise**.

Lorenzini, Carlo
(**Collodi**)
1826-1890
Lived 64yrs.

He was the author of **Pinocchio**. He was born in Florence. When he died he was buried at the church of **San Minato** that overlooks his beautiful city.

Medici, Lorenzo de'
1449-1492
Lived 43yrs.

He was the ruler of Florence; called **The Magnificent**. His family owned a bank. In 1478 the Pazzi family tried to assassinate him. They chased him and his brother, Giuliano age 25, into the Duomo Santa Maria del Fiore. Lorenzo escaped, but his brother was killed in the church.

Nutria
Live in the Arno River

They are cousin to the beaver, and similar in size. They have webbed feet and a rat-like tail.

Pazzi Family
Rich and powerful

They were a noble Florentine family who hated the Medici family and assassinated Giuliano de' Medici in the church Santa Maria del Fiore in 1478.

Plato
428(?)-347 B.C.
Lived~81yrs.

He was a Greek philosopher and mathematician. He was a student and friend of Socrates. As a teacher, he taught Aristotle; practiced alchemy.

Robbia, Luca della
1400(?)-1482
Lived~82yrs.

He used colored glazed terra-cotta in his sculptures, which can be found sprinkled all over the city of Florence. He is very famous for his **ten tondos**, or round sculptures, known as the "**Foundling Children**," on the Spedale degli Innocenti (Hospital of the Innocents), an ancient orphanage. These can be found near Piazza San Marco in **Piazza dell'Annuziata** in Florence, Italy.

Savonarola, Girolamo
1452-1498
Lived 46yrs.

He lived in the **monastery** of **San Marco** in **Piazza San Marco**, in the city of Florence. He was a Dominican priest who got involved in politics. He was excommunicated by the church, and found guilty of heresy in the civil courts. He was hanged, and then burned at the stake in **Piazza della Signoria**. In the piazza there is a large brass seal that commemorates his death.

The Plague
1348~1351

The Black Death, as it was called, arrived in Florence in 1348. A contemporary of the time, Giovanni Boccaccio writes about the suffering of the Florentine people and massive loss of life in his book **The Decameron**. It is believed that by 1351 nearly three quarters of the population in Florence had died.

Vinci, Leonardo da
1452-1519
Lived 67yrs

He was an architect, artist, engineer, painter, sculptor, and a scientist. He is still considered one of the greatest intellectuals of all time. His most famous painting is the "**Mona Lisa**", and she is on view in Paris, France, in the Louvre Museum. His other great work is "**The Last Supper**", and it is painted on a wall in the church at **Santa Maria delle Grazie** in Milan, Italy.

Vitruvius, Marcus Pollio
70(?)-25 B.C.

He was an architect and engineer; he served under the first Roman emperor, Augustus. He wrote the oldest surviving books on architecture and engineering.

Table of Contents

Introduction

By Zachari Nathanson

A warning bell sounded aboard the plane, signaling the passengers to take their seats and buckle up. A mom jumped from her seat, and dashed to the bathroom, leaving her two young sons joyfully playing side by side. In the row behind the brothers sat a lady, and she began to speak to them.

"Hi! Excuse me gentlemen, but the plane will be landing in about half an hour," the lady informed them. "I can see that your mom is stuck in a long line, and while she's away, I thought you boys could help her out. You have a bunch of stuff under your seats that might be important to you. You need to collect it, and pack it up. Many of your things slid onto my side during the flight. I can see pens and paper, and a puzzle book at my feet." The lady gathered them up, and handed them to the boys.

1

Peeking through a crack in the seats, the blond haired little boy just stared at the lady while she spoke. His green eyes sparkled with excitement as she leaned over, and handed the boys their things. He was mesmerized by a sparkling necklace that dangled between him and his brother. The little boy could hardly wait for the lady to finish what she was saying when he blurted out...

"Gee! That's a really cool necklace. Is it a robot?"

"No, but thank you. It's Bischero (Bee ska row), and he's made of silver. See how his body moves, his head, his arms and his legs. I found him while I was in Florence, Italy. Did you know that's where Bischero was born?"

"You mean that Bischero is real?" said the little boy.

"But, of course, and even though he was born many centuries ago, he still lives today, and that is how I was able to obtain this beautiful handmade pendant of him. Would you like to hear the story of what happened to Bischero as he was growing up?"

"Yes, please. My name is Zachari and this is my big brother Joshua." Twisting in his seat to face his brother, little Zach shouted enthusiastically, "Josh, did you know that Bischero is real? This lady is going to tell us all about him!"

CHAPTER ONE
The History of Bischero

There is an Irish proverb that says, "You must know where you come from to know who you are." During mediaeval times in the year 1498, Bischero (Bee ska row) was born without a name in an enchanted land, where hounds were kings and horses queens. It was a place where no one died but passed onto the Other World, a place of shape-shifters and song writers. The Land of the Druids is where he was born, and at that time the druids were the most powerful people in the land. They served the community and administered justice. Some were doctors and lawyers, while others were craftsmen and peacemakers.

The musicians were called Bards and traveled over the countryside singing the tales of ancient Celtic clans. Their history was told in the lyrics, and epic sagas were woven into song. They sang of how a people of old came to an emerald isle. The music they played, and the songs they sang nurtured and made sacred her soil. Today she is called Ireland. It is from these ancient folk, from so long ago, that Bischero descended.

Bischero's family was very noble, and they were embarrassed to have such a funny looking babe. He was small, wrinkled, and red, and for this reason they would not give him a name. By the time the babe was four years old he was still unable to speak, but he had grown into a very handsome child indeed. He had blond hair, and soft brown eyes that sparkled with a touch of gold and green that warmed a body's heart just to look at them. The druid couple loved their child deeply, but could not find a way to make him talk so they sent him to live with an old friend of the family who resided in Florence, Italy, for he had special abilities.

The day the child left Ireland he was dressed in the finest clothes made of golden threads. His mother gave him a sack of food, and a fresh round loaf of hot bread that she had just removed from the hearth. As he held it in his arms it warmed his small body against the chill of the ocean breeze. His father added some goat cheese and a bottle of warm fresh milk that came straight from the cow's utter. Then sadly his parents handed Bischero over to the ship's captain. The captain was given strict instructions on how to care for the child, and was handed a small map that marked the way to the house of their friend Giuseppe.

A bag of gold was placed into the palm of the sturdy sea captain, and the druids hugged their child for the last time as they said a tearful good-bye.

Four nights later the ship arrived in Florence by way of the Arno River. The child was cradled and sleeping in the arms of the sea captain when he was delivered to his new home, unaware that he had arrived. When he awoke in the morning, he found himself in a warm bed with a cozy fire to greet him. The glowing embers popped and crackled a welcoming tune. Groggy and lost in sleep, it took a few moments for the child to realize that he was no longer aboard the ship. He was alone and frightened. He did not know where he was, but when his stomach growled from emptiness, he knew he was hungry.

His hunger grew. It fed his courage, and aroused his curiosity. He slid down the side of the bed and stretched his toes long until they brushed the ground. When he was sure that he would not fall, he let go of the covers and firmly landed on both feet. The cold from the wooden floor touched against his bare skin and made him shiver. Quickly he looked around until he found a door. He had to stretch up high to reach the handle and he could barely get a finger-hold on it. Down went the handle, and slowly he opened the door. Just a crack, to see the room on the other side, and then the door sprang open. The child saw nothing, and the next instant a fuzzy little cat pressed through the opening and spiraled around his feet.

"Miscia (Me sha), Miscia (Me sha)," a man called in a soft voice.

Following the source of the voice, the boy looked up and found himself face to face with an old man. He was stunned from the sudden shock of meeting the man's gaze, and he could not move. The tension eased from the boy as he realized that he was staring into the kindest face he had ever seen. Like a clear diamond, the old man's eyes twinkled with sparkling bits of blue. He had crinkles in the corners of his eyes, and a stubbly beard. He had lots of hair for an old man, too. It was white and fell into deep waves from the top of his head and stopped at his shoulders. He chuckled and smiled at the half sleepy little boy who had one eye opened and one eye closed, and whose hair was sticking straight up on top. The old man was filled with the kind of joy you experience when you wake up on Christmas morn and discover the wonderful presents Santa has brought just for you. In a stream of flowing melody, the old man began to speak in a strange language that the boy had never heard. It had a musical rhythm that enchanted him, and as time passed from days to weeks, and weeks to months, the boy was able to understand that this man was called Giuseppe Lorenzini (Ju zep pay Lauren zee knee).

Those next few months were very hard on the boy because he had to learn to eat new foods that tasted spicy and tickled his tongue. Learning to eat spaghetti was particularly hard. Giuseppe had fun teaching Bischero how to twirl his spaghetti around a fork. Every time Bischero tried to lift the fork to his mouth, the ball of spaghetti would plop down onto his plate. He thought he would go hungry before he would ever learn how to get it into his mouth. He finally gave up and forked some long pieces into his mouth and sucked them in like giant worms.

The tomato sauce went flying in every direction. Some flew over and hit Giuseppe on the nose, and some sprayed across the table and landed on Miscia's furry face. She blinked and shook her head; she did not know what had hit her. Each time Bischero would suck down another noodle he and Giuseppe would laugh so hard that it took them an hour to eat their dinner. When Bischero was finished, he had tomato sauce all over his face and down the front of his shirt. Giuseppe understood how difficult it was to learn to eat spaghetti properly. Sometimes he would make macaroni for Bischero so that he could eat with a spoon. In time, Bischero learned how to spin his spaghetti to just the right size and just the right shape so that he could pop it into his mouth without a splash. But, he still liked to suck down a long string of spaghetti and lick off the sauce and Parmesan cheese mixture that gathered in a circle around his lips. It was fun! He was learning to be a real Italian!

As the months passed and a year went by, Bischero became captivated with the Italian language and the music that lived in the rhythm of the people's words. However, he still could not speak, nor could he understand all the words of this strange new language. For this reason the other children called him Bischero, which means "fool" in Florentine dialect, and that is how he got his name. Of course Bischero did not know what his name meant, but he was simply happy to have friends to play with, and proud to finally have a real name.

One day, Bischero was feeling sad because he missed his mother and father. They were getting harder to remember. Their faces were blurred in his memory.

He could not get them to shape clearly in his mind so that he could see their eyes, or their faces smile. It was hard to remember his old home. Then he would think of Giuseppe. Giuseppe made Bischero happy, and it seemed as though Giuseppe had loved him always. Bischero was adjusting slowly, and he was beginning to feel really happy in this new land. His parents promised him that they would be together again, so he tried to be brave and he dried his tears.

Later that night Giuseppe had a surprise birthday party for him. He did not know how old he was, or what a birthday party was all about. Giuseppe invited all the neighbor children to their house for a spaghetti dinner, Bischero's favorite, and the children brought him presents. It was December 15th. Bischero was five years old and excited to learn the day of his birth, but he was more eager to experience his first birthday party. He was so happy that he did not know what to do, and so he tried to talk. When he opened his mouth to try and say "thank you" to his Papa, words sprang out like musical notes. "Grazie mille, Papa!" (Graw zee A mee lay, Pa pa!") Everyone cheered, and then they sang "Happy Birthday" to Bischero:

"Tante auguri a te,
("Tawn tee ow gu ry aa tay,)
Tanti auguri a te,
Tanti auguri,
Tanti auguri,
Tanti auguri a te."

8

At five years old Bischero was able to go to school with the rest of the children. He was slower than most of them because he had not been talking long, but he did not mind because he knew he would soon catch up to the other children. He was happy to be learning new things. School is a place of learning, and it was there that he learned the legend of his name.

In the city of Florence there once lived a family by the name of "Bischeri" (Bee ska ree). Everyone knew them because they were kind and generous. They always spoke well of other people, and would give money to the poor. It was said that they never uttered a bad word, and that anyone who was in trouble could go to them and they would surely help. Not everyone loved the Bischeri family. There were some who were jealous of their wealth and charity. They wanted to see the Bischeri family without a florin (Florentine money of the time). Pietro Pazzi (<u>Pee ate row</u> <u>Pot zee</u>) happened to be one of these people. He came from a powerful Florentine home. He was very smart and realized that the kindness and generosity of the Bischeri family was their weakness, and he saw it as a way to make them lose all their money and power.

During these times, called the Renaissance, it was common for wealthy families to build beautiful churches near their homes for the people who supported their community. Pietro decided he would convince the Bischeri family that they should have the largest and most beautiful church in all of Florence, and because the Bischeri family trusted Pietro as a friend, unaware that he was truly their enemy, they accepted his council as wise and wanted to contribute to their beautiful city.

No expense was spared, and by the end of a year the family had spent almost all their wealth to build the church, and yet it still was not finished. The Bischeri family was in financial difficulty: they had no more money.

Now, any peasant would think that Pietro Pazzi's  jealousy would have been satisfied knowing that he was the one who destroyed the strength of the Bischeri family, but legend tells Pietro was an evil man. One night, Pietro set the church on fire and watched it burn to the ground and his laughter could be heard echoing through the small streets like a ghost riding on the wind. Well, from that day forward the people called Pietro Pazzi "crazy", and from that day to this, if a person is called "pazzo", then everyone knows it means that he is crazy. As for the Bischeri family, their name, too, became a slang term that means "fool", because they were foolish to trust a stranger, and spend all of their money. From that day to this, if a person is called "Bischero", then everyone knows it means he is a simple-minded fool.

Bischero was proud that everyone thought him to be kind and trusting like the Bischeri family, even though he was a little simple-minded. The children loved him and were good to him. He did not get upset because his name could also be meant as fool, and he promised himself that someday his name would work to his advantage and bring honor to him and the Bischeri family.

Life in Florence passed with great joy, and Bischero was proud of his foster father Giuseppe. Giuseppe came from a long line of puppeteers who mostly lived in the small town outside of Florence, called Collodi.

Although Giuseppe did not make puppets, he did make wonderful toys of every shape, size and color. So when Bischero was by himself, he could play with anything he wanted, but he liked playing with Giuseppe's poor little cat Miscia best. She was a beautiful cat with just the right amount of black and white in all the right places, but she always seemed to have a terrible cold. She would sneeze repeatedly, and when she slept at night she snored. Most of the kids would tease her, and they refused to play with her because she made gross sounds that gurgled just before a large thick green string of slimy snot would squirt out and dangle from her nose.

Bischero loved Miscia just as she was, and she loved him too. She would follow him everywhere he went until he left the house. Miscia was happy to stay at home by the warm fire. She had a hard time breathing when it was cold outside, and she did not like the kids teasing her. She preferred to stay inside, and watch the world from her favorite spot at the window. She would jump on the windowsill, so she could see Bischero as he walked down the street. She would stay there until he vanished from sight, and without fail, Bischero would find her waiting in the window for him when he returned. Somehow, she always knew when Bischero was coming home; often he would see her from the street as he approached his tiny home. She craned her neck like a bird on the lookout to get a glimpse of him; it was like she could read his mind and knew that he was near.

Then, one cold day in May, when Bischero was eight years old, in the year 1507, the weather in Florence was changing from winter to spring. The skies grew dark with thunderous rain clouds as Bischero stood watching from a tiny window that looked onto the Florentine streets.

11

He was very nervous and scared because Giuseppe was ill. Bischero's neighbor went to get the city doctor, but it seemed as though the doctor would never come. "What could be taking them so long?" he thought. Just then, the wind began to howl and blow with furry, and at a distance Bischero could see his neighbor, Leonardo da Vinci. He was coming around the corner, and with him was a strange looking man. The man was dressed in a black cape and hood that made Bischero tremble. He had never seen a doctor before, and he thought this man looked more like death coming to his door, than a doctor who could heal his loving father.

Bischero ran to the door to let in the doctor and Leonardo. Leonardo had to help little Bischero close the door because the wind was so fierce he did not have the strength to close it by himself.

Bischero felt afraid because a black hood was draped over the head of the doctor, and it shrouded his face in a black void. It made the doctor appear ghostly, and Bischero wondered if the man could really help his father. Without saying a word and hanging his head low, he showed the doctor to Giuseppe's bedroom. The black doctor would not let Bischero stay inside the room with Giuseppe. In silence, the cloaked figure raised his arm and pointed to the door. So he had to wait outside his father's bedroom. This made Bischero feel he was a stranger in his own home.

Leonardo would not leave Bischero's side and tried to give him words of encouragement, but Bischero could not stop thinking about the hard feeling in his stomach that made him ache.

It was like a rock, Bischero felt all hope was gone; he just did not want to believe it. The rock in his stomach told him the doctor would not have good news about his father.

After what seemed a very long time, the doctor came out of Giuseppe's room with his cloak pulled down around his shoulders. Bischero could see the man had a very kind face. His skin was smooth over his shining baldhead, and his face was full of wrinkles. His eyes were light blue and he had bushy eyebrows. When the man began to speak, Bischero discovered he had a most soothing voice, like a cool gentle breeze on a hot summer's day. Leonardo broke into the conversation and introduced the priest as Father Domenico (during this time all the doctors were priests, and it was their custom to dress in a black cloak and hood). Bischero felt much better. He was happy to learn the doctor was a man of God. Surely, he could make his papa well again.

Father Domenico said, "My dear little Bischero, it is a pleasure to meet you. I am sorry it has to be under these tragic circumstances. I can see you are a delightful child. You must bring Giuseppe great joy. Now, my son, you must be strong and have great courage. Go in and comfort your father. There is nothing more I can do for him. His life is in the hands of God."

"Come here, Bischero," Giuseppe said with a raspy voice that could hardly be heard over the roaring storm. "Do not be afraid, my son. I want to talk to you."

Then, in an instant, the wind stopped blowing and the clouds parted in the night sky.

13

Through the window of Giuseppe's bedroom shined a bright star that illuminated the entire room into a beautiful moonlight blue. It was so quiet Bischero felt he and his father were the only two people in the whole world. How very old and tired his father looked, he thought. Slowly Giuseppe began to speak.

"Bischero, you are my only child and I am so proud of you. You are still so very young. Can you please forgive this old man for leaving?"

"What do you mean, Father?" said Bischero. "Where are you going?"

"Oh! My poor little orphan, life is still too new for you to understand that one day a person's life must leave his body and go to live with God, the Almighty, in heaven above," continued Giuseppe. "God is the creator of all life and it has been through His grace that the spirit of life has filled your soul and given you a human form. You are God's greatest gift to me, and he must have made you with a special purpose in mind. Follow your heart and God will lead you down your special path of life. Trust in Leonardo and he will help guide you. He is my oldest and dearest friend. Be a good son to Leonardo, as you have been to me. Remember that I will always be with you, even though you may not see me. I love you, Bischero...," gasped Giuseppe with his last breath.

The small bedroom filled with a light so bright that Bischero blinked his eyes trying to see, but it was no use because the light was blinding. Then, the light streaked out the window and Bischero watched it soar into the evening sky. The light flew until it reached a shining star.

There was a great flash and the rain began to fall once more. Bischero was in shock. He could not believe his eyes. In his heart, Bischero knew that the glow of light he saw flying into the evening sky was his father's spirit. Now, Bischero understood where heaven must be and that Giuseppe was with God. When he turned to face his father's bed, he found Leonardo blocking the view where his father's body lay. With outstretched arms, Leonardo told Bischero to come to him and to be his son as he had been Giuseppe's.

CHAPTER TWO
Bischero Begins Another Life

Death is a part of life and it is hard to understand. Leonardo did his best to comfort Bischero (Bee ska row). He stood by his side as they buried Giuseppe (Ju zep pay) high upon the hill, in the church, at San Miniato (<u>San</u> <u>Mini aw toe</u>). From San Miniato Bischero could look down upon his father's beloved city of Florence. Bischero felt good knowing he had rested his father in such a beautiful place, and from this hilltop he was closer to heaven. If he wanted to talk to his father, he was sure he could hear him from this holy place of tranquility and sacred ground.

For some time Bischero walked over the hillside; from San Miniato he walked to Fort Belvedere (<u>Fort</u> <u>Bell va day ray</u>) and past the home of his friend Benvenuto Cellini (<u>Ben vay new toe</u> <u>Chel lee knee</u>).

16

Bischero did not feel like visiting with Benvenuto so he continued on his way to the Ponte Vecchio (<u>Pon tay Vec key oo</u>). He stood on the bridge for a while thinking of days from long ago, when he was carefree without a worry in the world; where he and his friend would often sing, play, and use their imaginations. He remembered Benvenuto saying how he would like to make a bronze statue of himself and place it on the bridge so that he would always be a part of the Ponte Vecchio, and so that the Florentine people would remember him through the centuries. Bischero wondered if the people would remember his papa. Then Bischero began to recite his favorite poem, it always made him feel happy inside:

> Sittin' her thinkin'
> Not causin' trouble,
> just contemplatin;
> Watchin' a frog on a lily pad
> Wastin' time really ain't so bad
> Bumps and knots
> and owl's in the tree
> There's a squirrel lookin'
> down at me
> Crickets jump and eagles fly
> It must be fun soarin' so high
> Sittin' here thinkin'
> Not causin' trouble,
> just contemplaltin'

Instead of feeling happy, Bischero shivered with fear, "What will happen to me? Once my papa was young like me, and then he grew old. I do not want to die, but I am afraid to live without my papa."

17

A soft wind blew whispering into Bischero's ear. It gave him an idea. Bischero jumped down from his perch and ran to Leonardo's workshop by the Uffizi (Ou fee zee). The wind had told him that Leonardo would know what to do.

Bischero had never been inside the workshop of Leonardo da Vinci. He knew his friend was famous for his scientific mind and his great paintings, but to Bischero he was just Leonardo, his father's  best friend. The door to Leonardo's office faces the Arno River and once inside he was surprised to see a spiral staircase that led downwards. Once he reached the bottom, he opened a wooden door that led him to a grassy patch of earth just below the Uffizi. It was a heavenly spot, and was plain to see from the other side of the river. Why had he never noticed it before? It looked like a tiny island that stretched out to the Arno's watery edge, and at one end there was a small dock with a boat attached. Bischero found another door, but it was locked, so he thought he would wait a while to see if Leonardo would return. Patiently, Bischero sat on the bank of the Arno and looked at his reflection in the muddy water.

He was looking at himself in the reflection of the still water, when all of the sudden, and with great speed, up jumped a wet furry ball with a long rat-like tail. The creature collided into Bischero's face, and they tumbled backwards over each other. Then the furry creature froze. He did not move a whisker. He just sat there dripping and looking eye to eye with Bischero. It was hard to tell who was more afraid. Bischero was the first to speak.

"Hi! My name is Bischero. Do you want to be my friend?"

The dripping creature waddled to one side and replied, "I guess so. My name is Pasquale (Paw squal lay). Does Leonardo know you are here? Who are you? You are awfully small for a human, and you are funny looking too. You scared me."

"Oh, I am sorry I scared you, but you scared me too. I am just a boy, and I am here to see Leonardo; he is my new father. My real papa is in heaven and Leonardo wants to take care of me," explained Bischero. "So your name is Pasquale. How did you and Leonardo become friends?"

"It is a long story," Pasquale began. "I was born right here on this very spot three years ago. I am a nutria, and my kind lives in the Arno River. I am an orphan; I never knew my mama or my papa. Leonardo and Ghiberti (Ghee bear tee) were my only family. Ghiberti is a nutria too, but Ghiberti is mean and cruel, and he stole one of Leonardo's inventions. He has it hidden down below in the deep water of the Arno. But, I found it! I know its secret hiding place. I was coming to tell Leonardo."

"He is not here. I do not know where he is either," said Bischero. "I feel better knowing you, Pasquale. You make me feel happy inside. I am glad you are my friend."

"Can you swim?" asked Pasquale. "I will take you below and show you Ghiberti's fortress. Maybe you can help me get back Leonardo's invention, and together we can surprise him.

19

Since Leonardo is like my father too, I guess that makes us brothers."

"Sure, I can swim," said Bischero. "Let's go!"

With that they both jumped into the muddy waters of the Arno River. Bischero had forgotten he was human and his lungs needed air to breathe. Before he knew it, he was unconscious and floating up to the surface of the water. Bischero had drowned himself!

Quickly, Pasquale swam after Bischero and helped him onto the shore. Bischero lay limp on the ground like a wet rag. Then a bright light shone over the boy's lifeless body, and a man's voice spoke.

"Wake-up Bischero."

"Yes, Father," replied Bischero as though he were half asleep.

"You are being given a second chance at life, my son. When you first came to me you could not speak, and so there were many things you could not understand. As a human being you cannot plunge to the depths of the Arno, because your lungs must have air to breathe, and your life will end by nature's hand. If you choose to return to this land you will be able to change your form, because you are a druid. In time you will learn more of what this means, but for now you will be able to help Leonardo, and the children who need you. What do you say, Bischero?" asked the voice of Giuseppe.

"Yes, Father. I want to help Leonardo, and I want to be like you. I want to love the children, make them laugh and see them smile," replied Bischero.

The light that shined over Bischero became so bright that Pasquale had to squeeze his eyes really tight. When he opened them again, Bischero stood as a boy made of oak, just like one of Giuseppe's toys. Something about the way Bischero looked made him seem older to Pasquale. Then, Bischero began to speak.

"Oh! Pasuqale, I am so happy. I have a purpose in my life. I am going to help people and make them happy too. I understand how important one person can be, and now I know my papa will always be with me, even though I cannot see him or talk to him–he is watching over me. My papa loves me. He taught me how to create great joy. Life is the greatest, most wondrous gift. You know, Pasquale, I may not be very smart but I feel all grown-up," declared Bischero.

"You look a whole year older! I can see that you are made of wood, but you look so real," exclaimed Pasquale.

Indeed it was true. Bischero bent down to the water's edge and saw his reflection. He knocked on his head, and sure enough, he heard an echo. Except for a few changes he still looked like a real live boy. When he held his hand out straight in front of him, he could see the grains of wood and bolted joints that linked his fingers together. Just then, Leonardo came into view. Bischero explained how he had drowned and came back to life again.

21

"Well," said Leonardo. "That is quite a story. Now, come into my workshop because I want to give you something very special."

CHAPTER THREE
Bischero Learns a Secret

Inside of Leonardo's workshop, Bischero (Bee ska row) saw such wonderful things. Crowded together on the floor stood several paintings propped up against the wall. In one corner stood a painting easel with a half-drawn picture of an angel talking to the face of a beautiful lady: "The Annunciation". On a small bench were various sizes of paint brushes and a small flat piece of wood that had all kinds of bright colors mixed in tiny swirls. As Bischero was looking about, he found a book with funny writing. It had a strange drawing of a man with his arms stretched out over his head, and his feet were spread apart forming his body into the shape of an "X."

The whole body was enclosed with a perfect circle touching only the tips of the longest fingers and the bottom of the man's feet.

Bischero studied the picture for some time, but could not understand the picture's meaning. Leonardo watched Bischero's curiosity with enthusiasm, knowing he had made the right choice in selecting Bischero to guard his greatest secret. Then Leonardo walked over to Bischero and explained the significance of his drawing.

"Do you see how I have drawn a perfect circle around the man, Bischero?" asked Leonardo. "I call him the Vitruvian Man after the great Roman architect Vitruvius."

"Yes," replied Bischero, "but what does it mean?"

"You are wiser than you know Bischero. Most people would not understand that my drawing has any significance. It is one of my scientific discoveries. First, I took many measurements of the human body. Then, when I made my drawing, I realized I was able to form a perfect circle around the body. This proves that the length of a man's arms from the longest point of his left hand to the longest point of his right hand is equal to his height from the tip of his head to the bottom of his feet," explained Leonardo.

"What is this strange writing?" asked Bischero.

"Haa!" exclaimed Leonardo. "I had to develop a secret code to write in, otherwise if someone were to read my notes they might think I was a mad man, or worse, a witch to be burned at the stake."

24

"You mean like the way Savonarola (Saw von aa roll aa) was burned at the stake in Piazza Della Signoria (<u>Pee aught zaw</u> <u>Day la</u> <u>Sin your ree aa</u>)?" questioned Bischero.

"Savonarola was a monk who became involved in Florentine politics, and when his side lost the fight

they burned him in the square to frighten anyone else who may have considered going against the Medici (May dee chee) family in the future. Savonarola was used as an example. Today,

you will find a large brass seal located in front of Neptune's fountain displaying the exact point where the monk was condemned at the stake. No, Bischero, I do not wish to be accused of ignorant lies, nor did I want anyone to steal my research. So, I

wrote all my notes backwards so no one else could read them. If you ever need to read my notes just hold them up to a mirror. You will find that all the words will turn around in the right order so that you will be able to make sense of them.

Now you know one of my secrets Bischero. What I truly need is to trust you with my most important secret. Can I believe in you and place my trust in you, Bischero?" asked Leonardo in a very serious tone of voice.

Bischero stood really tall with his shoulders back and said, "Yes, Sir! You can count on me."

Turning to Pasquale, Leonardo inquired, "Have you found Ghiberti's fortress, and secret hiding place?"

"Yes, he is hiding your invention in a cave of rose-colored limestone," responded Pasquale with reverence.

"Good. Then you and Bischero must team up with Donato (Doe not toe). Go to his palace and ally yourselves with him and his men. Donato has a great mind, and is very cunning on the battlefield. That is why he is called, 'The Magnificent'. Tell him to have some of his men attack Ghiberti's fortress and create a distraction. In the meantime, Donato can take you boys and a few of his best men to the cave of rose-colored limestone to destroy my invention.

"Listen and listen well my children, Leonardo continued. This is a dangerous mission that I have bestowed upon you. You must take heed. Ghiberti has become very powerful. He was an innocent nutria by nature, but he became a cruel creature because of the experiments I conducted on him. It is my fault he has fallen victim to man's bad example. I did not understand the consequences of my actions. I gave him a potion to stimulate his brain, and produced intellectual awareness. Knowledge is a great source of power, and if used improperly it can be worse than the great plague that ravaged our beautiful city in 1348. So, you see it is my fault Ghiberti has become the monster he is today. I gave him too much knowledge. I do not want Ghiberti hurt. Instead, after you have won the battle, have Donato banish Ghiberti from the Arno forever. But first, you must destroy my invention in front of Ghiberti's own eyes. You must convince Ghiberti that it is destroyed forever.

26

He knows my invention is powerful and he will not leave until he knows all hope for learning its secrets has been snuffed out. Ghiberti is very smart, but he did not observe me long enough to understand how to use my invention. Given time, I believe he will figure it out. My fear is that he may have already learned its secrets. I hope we are not too late."

CHAPTER FOUR
Bischero Begins His Dangerous Quest

Pushing back a stone against the wall, Leonardo reached into a small hole and pulled out a purple pouch that contained one gold coin. The coin seemed ordinary enough. It had the face of Lorenzo de' Medici (<u>Lauren zo</u> <u>day</u> <u>May</u> <u>dee chee</u>) on the front and the Florentine lily on the back. The only thing different about the coin was that it was in the shape of an octagon with eight flat edges instead of being a smooth, round circle.

He placed the pouch in Bischero's hand and said, "Please step into my office and close the door. What I have to say is for your ears and yours alone, Bischero (Bee ska row)."

Patiently Pasquale (Paw squal lay) waited in the workroom while Leonardo and Bischero spoke to each other in privacy. After what seemed a very long time, Bischero emerged from the office. Together, he and Pasquale swam downward into the Arno, toward the palace of The Magnificent. They would begin their quest from there.

Plunging into the depths of the Arno, Bischero followed Pasquale to Donato's palace. The water was murky brown, mixed with the silt from the river bottom. It was difficult for Bischero to see. He swam hard to stay close to Pasquale, fearful he might get lost. Nutria have a keen sense of sight in the darkness, and Bischero trusted his friend to guide him in the right direction. After a few minutes, Bischero could no longer see the light shining downwards from the water's surface. In fact, he could not tell which way was up or which way was down. At last, he and Pasquale broke through the surface of the water. Here the air was damp and musty, but safe to breathe. Nutrias are mammals, which means they have lungs and need air, or they too can drown. They have webbed feet, which are designed for swimming, and with Pasquale's wide shaped feet he leapt out of the water with ease.

Bischero found himself at the bottom of a fountain that sprung into a beautiful garden. This was the secret entrance into the Palazzo D'Ambra. The fountain was very simple and more closely resembled an oval pond or wishing well.

It was made from the finest white Carrara marble, and because of the smooth sides, Bischero had a hard time climbing out of the fountain. He fell back into the water with a big splash! He made such a loud noise that an echo bounced around the room. From nowhere a large nutria with a sword rushed toward them, running with the swiftness of the wind. His feet were motorized, and his heart pounded fiercely against his chest. He was ready for attack.

When the large nutria recognized his friend Pasquale, he came to a sudden stop. His face transformed into a wide smile as he welcomed him with warm affection. Bischero was so overwhelmed with fright that he fell backwards into the fountain for a second time. Pasquale and his friend broke into giant laughter, and then they each took Bischero by a hand and pulled him from the chilly pond.

It took a few minutes for Bischero's eyes to adjust to the change of light. As Bischero glanced around he could see specks of light dancing off flecks of amber and gold. Eventually Bischero was able to see that they were not really precious stones, but rather strands of straw that had been woven together. It was like being inside the largest basket Bischero had ever seen. The ground was covered with soft, mossy green grass, and bordering the edge were the tiniest of flowers. The flowers adorned the surroundings in all shades of blues, yellows, reds, pinks, and purples. The air felt velvety and floated against Bischero's body. When he looked up, he guessed that the light source cascading downwards must somehow be the sun. Bischero wondered, how did it reach through the murky surface from so high above to place a glow so far below? Bischero felt like he was in a dream.

Once Bischero caught his balance, Pasquale introduced him to Donato, The Magnificent. Donato stood very regal and erect, his shoulders straight and his head held high. He wore his black hair tied in a long ponytail at the back of his neck. His face was very rugged looking, framed with long side burns, a mustache, and a beard. Bischero imagined that the females must think him quite handsome and comely. He liked Donato instantly, realizing that he possessed all the qualities necessary to be a good leader and to run a kingdom.

Donato began to speak "Welcome to Palazzo D'Ambra, Bischero. I did not mean to frighten you with my sword, but you caught me in the middle of my fencing lesson. We D'Ambras don't use the crude and ancient method of sword fighting for protection any longer, although we do respect the skill and art of fencing–it's good exercise. It takes a skilled hand and a keen mind to outwit your opponent; it is very challenging. Well, enough of that. Since you used my private entrance, you must be here on urgent business. How can I be of assistance?"

Pasquale and Bischero took turns explaining the situation. Donato thought it would be safest to have Pasquale and Bischero spend the night in the palace until he could gather his men and formulate a plan for the morrow.

During the night, Bischero was woken by the sound of someone tapping. Slowly, he crept through the palace halls following the pinging echo until he found his way into a sculptor's workroom. There were large chunks of marble scattered all over the floor.

In the far corner, with a chisel in his hand, stood Donato hammering away at a life-size statue. It was too dark for Bischero to see what he was working on. Donato stopped and draped a cloth over his sculpture. Bischero hid behind a large piece of white Carrara marble and watched Donato as he knelt before the statue and began to weep. After a few minutes, Donato slowly stood up, blew out the light, and left the workshop. Bischero was very curious. He had to find out what was under the cloth that could make such a strong person cry.

It was hard for Bischero to see in the shadows, and it was important to be quiet. He did not want Donato to discover him. Stepping with great care, it seemed an hour had passed before he finally reached the hidden statue across the room, and just as he was reaching for the cloth he twisted his ankle and crashed onto the floor. Buried under the weight of the cloth, Bischero uncovered himself to find he was nose to nose with Donato.

"What have you done?" cried Donato

"I am sorry," apologized Bischero. "I could not help it. My curiosity got the best of me. I had to remove the cloth to see the statue. Why was she hidden? She is so beautiful. Why have you not finished sculpting her face? Who is she?"

"My young lad, you have discovered the suffering of my heart," said Donato. "Because you mourn the loss of your father, I shall share with you my heartache. You are young, but it is time you learn that there are many ways to lose someone you love, and death is not the only avenue.

"Long ago, I fell in love with a beautiful young lady. She was the daughter of a common merchant. She was charming, bright, and educated. Nevertheless, she was not of noble birth. Our love was doomed from the start. You see, I am of the Nobility, and it is not allowed for us to marry beneath our station. If I had married her, I would have lost my home, my position, and my family."

"Is there nothing you could have done to keep her?" questioned Bischero.

"No, and yes. If I had chosen to marry with a commoner, I would have lost my riches," explained Donato. "Would she have loved me then, I had asked myself? The answer was Yes, Bischero. My Lady was an angel of a woman. She believed in me. She knows that I was a strong man and I could have made a life for us.

"Today there are the modern thoughts of the young, who would have supported me and helped me keep all I am entitled to from birth. Then, there are others who are locked in ancient tradition and would never approve. Among them are the members of my family and the Church."

"What happened to this Lady? What is her name?" asked Bischero.

"She is called, Gianna (Jon aa). She has a heart of gold, and is the gentlest of creatures. All those who know her are touched by her loving spirit," Donato said, as his eyes drifted off to a faraway place. His body was present, but his mind traveled a great distance, as though he was not really with Bischero.

"Gianna could not bear the heartache of living in the same city with me," continued Donato. "So, she ran away to the South of France. When she left, with her, she took my heart. Without her, my heart is empty and what you see is only a shell of a being that looks like a king."

"I know what you are thinking Bischero," anticipated Donato. "There are many who have told me that I should never have let her go and believe I am a most stupid man. They believe I should go after her and bind her to me in matrimony, so that I can keep her with me forever. But, I was clear with Gianna from the start. I told her she could not have what she wanted most–a life together with me. I understand that is no excuse and it did not stop me from falling in love with her either. I only knew I could not live without my worldly possessions, or my family, and now it seems I must live without my heart. Somehow it made more sense that the two of us should suffer the grief of broken hearts, rather than make my entire family live with the consequences of my actions.

"She was my greatest treasure of all, but I lost her because of my selfish greed. The only way I could honor my family and keep Gianna with me forever was to make a statue of her. I could not bear her eyes looking down upon me each day, and so, I did not have the courage to finish her sweet face. It was my shame that stopped me from finishing her features, and the reason why her face will remain blank.

"I am a leader among my people, and no one must know the tender secret of my heart. I am Donato, The Magnificent! Bischero, you must swear an oath of silence, to never tell another living creature of my secret," commanded The Magnificent.

Thoughtfully, The Magnificent began. "Bischero, you are the only person I know with your unique skin color that looks like wood. God must have a special purpose in mind for you, and I believe that you should learn wisdom. From my story I hope that you have learned that leaders of men also have hearts. Sometimes, we must make difficult choices, which leave us alone and distance us from others. Sometimes we make mistakes, and then we must suffer the consequences of our errors. Doing the right thing does not always mean doing what we want, because we must consider those around us and how our actions will affect our family and friends. That is called 'acting responsibly'. Making choices can hurt, and that is why there are many other ways to mourn in this life, other than grieving over the death of a loved one. When we are in doubt, we must look deep within ourselves to find the answers."

Bischero did not really understand what The Magnificent was trying to say to him, but he felt honored to be spoken to as his equal and a friend. Then he returned to his room. Bischero was so tired that he fell asleep before his head rested on the pillow, and instantly he started to dream . . .

CHAPTER FIVE
Bischero Dreams of a Sacred Land

Bischero (Bee ska row) found himself surrounded by a thick fog. He felt neither cold nor wet from the dew, and yet the mist continued to swirl around him without any weight or substance. Everywhere he looked, all he could see was white. He should feel afraid, he thought, but instead he felt calm and peaceful. His instincts told him that he should wait for someone to come to him, and after a few moments his eyes focused on a figure taking shape in the fog. The mist twisted and rolled until it formed a long white robe, and a man stepped forward. He was of medium height with broad shoulders. His golden hair was long and tightly curled. Bischero could see that he was not young, but nor was he old, he appeared middle-aged.

His face was smooth, and the corners of his green eyes puckered with joy. Although his robe hung loosely, Bischero could see that the man had muscular shoulders, and he imagined that he must be very strong.

In a mild but firm voice the man spoke, "Hello Bischero. Welcome to the mound of Amfwyn. My name is Colin and I am a druid just like you. You are now eight and a year, and it is time for you to learn more about your homeland of Ireland, and what being a druid means to our world."

The fog parted, and the stars shined brightly in the night sky. Under Bischero's feet lay soft green grass that formed a hump on the land. The hills rolled out in front of him, and he could see a waterfall cascading into an endless valley; behind him ebbed a calm sea, and it sent him a breeze. This place made Bischero feel as if he stood on the threshold of time. He could see the future that lay before him, and the past that stood behind him. His heart told him that all things were possible in the world, and that he was a part of it all.

"The druids are a special group," Colin began anew. "We sprang from the Celtic people and are spread across the Irish countryside. Our clans are ancient and can be found in every nation. By the age of four our children are sent to live with other clans, as you have been. This is done so that our children can develop a love and understanding for other people outside of their own. By age thirteen they return to their native lands. This creates a bond which unites the outlying clans. We have sworn to protect each other during the hard times, and it keeps us at peace.

When there is a drought so that the fields will not grow, and a famine so that our people go hungry, our clans come together. One clan may have a large store of grain, or another a river that runs through their land. We join together to help those who have not. One day, or another, those who give will also be the ones who need, and so the seasons cycle and our people grow.

"Through the ages we have learned to recognize when a druid child is born. They are always very special, and stand out from other children, as you did when you were a babe. You were small, wrinkled and red. Sure enough, you were as homely a child as I had ever seen. But later, as you grew, you developed quite handsomely indeed. Your blond hair shone yellow from the sun. Your soft brown eyes sparkled with flakes of gold, and with just a touch of Irish green for good luck. For all the changes you made, you were still unable to speak. When we were able to see that you could not, or would not speak, well, this was the third sign that you were truly a druid. Druid children always seem to have what others may call a handicap, but we know that it is only a mask to cover the greatness that lay inside.

"You are lucky, too, because you come from a noble family. It is a rare gift for a druid to come from nobility. Most descend from families that are dirt poor, who work hard at toiling the soil to feed their offspring. You have descended from Lugh of The Long Hand. He was a great and powerful king, who had special gifts and whose power reached beyond time and space. For this reason you are an oddity, but because of it, you will do great deeds.

"The day will come when you shall return to Ireland, and then you will learn much more of your great heritage.

It is said that you must know where you come from to know who you are. In Ireland you will also find many mysteries, but only because you are a druid will you see what lay before you. You see, only a druid can hear the sacred stone cry, or pass to and fro' the Other World. It is here that you can stand on the sacred mound of Amfwyn. The mound will grant the wish of a pure heart, but if you have an evil heart it will punish you with your own hatred. These are the legacies of the ancients that have passed from one generation to the next. In time, you will have the need for all these things, but for now you must learn the gift of the music that lives within your own heart.

"Each druid possesses the gift of music. It is a blessing that can lift the spirits of mankind and change the way the flowers grow. Listen to the sound of your heart and discover the rhythm that flows like the river of time itself. When you are one with your heart, you will find your power and control your destiny. Do you see how you are one with the oak tree? Well, do not look so astonished, Bischero. You look like the mighty oak because it stands strong and tall. It is a great symbol of our people. Now, concentrate and unlock the power that was created in your brain, and passed down from the first man to you. You must merge the right and left hemispheres of the brain together so that they are working as one. Listen to the rhythm of your heart. See yourself separate from the oak, instead of living inside its core, as you are now."

Bischero did as he was told. He closed his eyes and listened to his heart beat like a metronome. Tick, tock, tick, tock . . . From the distance a melody began to form in his mind; he felt weightless and free. He concentrated hard on the music until he could see the mighty oak standing before him.

When he looked down upon his hand, he could see that it was as it had been before his drowning. His skin was the color of cream, and no longer had the look of an oak tree. He was restored.

"In the beginning, man was one with the animals, but when man became filled with pride he was separated from nature's garden. The road map to return is locked within each of us, and as a druid you have the ability to find your way back. We are here to teach, and to serve. It is also a druid's responsibility to bring out the good in mankind, and to show him that all things are possible. We must never give up hope. You have all of Nature at your disposal, and it will assist you along your journey. The animals are your friends, and colleagues. You will be able to speak with them, and they with you. You will run like a stallion, swim like a salmon, and fly like the dove, but only if you listen to the music of your heart. Now, the dawn is coming and I must part, but we shall meet again. Dream sweet dreams little Bischero, and awake to your destiny..."

Colin faded into the foggy mist, and Bischero drifted back into a peaceful sleep.

CHAPTER SIX
The Battle

Early the next morning, Pasquale (Paw squal lay) rolled over on his back and stretched his body out until his toes were pointed in a straight line. He yawned and then shook himself from head to toe. Refreshed, he ambled down the hall toward Bischero's room.

Slowly he poked his head around the open archway to get a peek inside Bischero's room. Pasquale thought it would be fun to sneak up on Bischero (Bee ska row) while he was sleeping and scare him. But Pasquale's webbed feet were designed more for swimming than walking on tiptoes, and he tripped over his own feet. His body rolled up like a ball and he smashed into the sleeping boy.

"Gee, Pasquale.   Are you okay?" asked Bischero.

"Yah, I am okay, I am just a little embarrassed. I do not mean to be so clumsy, but my feet always seem to get in the way," said Pasquale. "Come on Bischero, it is time to meet Donato (Doe not toe) in the Great Hall. By now he should have gathered all of his men so that we can go after Ghiberti (Ghee bear tee)."

Bischero sat up in bed and the light streamed in from the open door and rested on his face. Pasquale stared at his friend's face and blinked in disbelief at what he saw. Then he said, "Bischero your face has changed. It does not look like an oak tree anymore. You have changed again."
Bischero remembered his dream, and realized that it was one of the mysteries that only a druid could understand.

"Pasquale, do not worry," he reassured. "I was visited in my dreams by a friend named Colin. He advised me to listen to my heart, because that's where my power lives. He helped me to understand that I am unique among men. He told me that I am a druid and I have special gifts. As a druid, it will be my responsibility to help others discover the secrets that lay within them. Now let's get going. We have a varmint to catch!"

Bischero jumped from his bed. He had slept in his clothes and was ready for action. He raced Pasquale to the Great Hall, but before they could enter they had to top and catch their breaths. It would not be proper to run in such a formal meeting room.

Once they had collected themselves, they prepared to make a grand entrance into the Great Hall. They breathed in deeply and pumped up their chests really high, just like true noblemen. They thought the hall would be full of courageous fighting men, so they were shocked when they only saw two men. Donato and his 1st in command, Mimmo (Mee moe). They wondered where all of Donato's men could be? Disappointed and as if defeated, they let the air out of their chests and fell back down to normal size. Looking at each other and shrugging their shoulders, they hoped that Donato and Mimmo had not noticed the spectacle they had made of themselves. They slumped over and resumed their normal stride, and continued walking toward the only two men in the room.

Mimmo's face was firm with concentration as he listened to Donato's tense voice echoing against the amber walls. As Bischero and Pasquale approached, Donato's keen sense of smell detected them before he was able to hear the sound of their footsteps. Each person has his or her own personal scent, so Donato knew exactly who had walked into the Great Hall. Donato called out to a palace servant and gave instructions for a quick breakfast to be served. Donato explained that he had sent his men ahead and they were waiting in position to receive Donato's command to advance.

They were served seeds and small plants for the first dish, and bird's eggs and small lizards for the main course. It was a breakfast fit for a king; well, "King of the River Nutria" in any case. Bischero's stomach growled with hunger. He longed for a croissant filled with jam or creamy custard, and a cup of hot chocolate to wash it down.

He watched as his three companions eagerly ripped and shredded their food into small pieces. As he watched his friends tear away at the dead and stinky lizards, one limb at a time, he grew sick to his stomach and lost his appetite. In a matter of moments every morsel was devoured. Nutria are omnivorous and will eat most any vegetation or decaying flesh. He did not wish to offend Donato's hospitality, so he excused himself by saying that he was too nervous to eat, and that he would have something when their mission was over.

Once breakfast was done, they returned to the secret entrance in Donato's garden. In one great leap they dove into the depths of the marble fountain. It was a long swim, and Pasquale took the lead so he could guide them to a hidden pocket of air near the entrance to Ghiberti's cave. If they could not reach the air pocket in time, they would all die.

Swiftly and gracefully, they all swam with great speed, except for Bischero. His hands and feet were not webbed for swimming like the others, so Mimmo had to keep an eye on him so he wouldn't get lost. When the others got too far ahead Mimmo would catch up to them, and with a sweeping gesture he would circle once around the group to let them know that Bischero was a far distance behind. Donato tried very hard to be patient, but he knew that time was of the essence, and if they did not reach the pocket of air soon they would all drown. Donato made a waving motion to Mimmo and the pair went back for Bischero. Each one took an arm and together they propelled Bischero forward in a blast of desperate energy. Time was running out.

Bischero was no longer made of wood, and his lungs needed air. He began to feel dizzy, and sleepy, because he was losing oxygen to his brain.

He was beginning to drown. Then, somewhere in the back of his mind, he could hear Colin's voice, "Listen to the music in your heart... You can swim like a salmon." The rhythm of Bischero's heart began to beat louder: tick, tock, tick, tock, like a metronome. In his mind he pictured a salmon, and he became the salmon. His eyes opened wide, he could breathe under water. Bischero was swimming on his own and with greater strength than Donato, Mimmo, or Pasquale. Bischero was now able to help his friends, and together he launched them forward at blinding speed to the lifesaving pocket of air.

When they finally reached the pocket, Pasquale, Donato, and Mimmo were gasping for air, but Bischero was strong and full of energy. Without thinking, Bischero transformed back into himself. He felt great, but it took the others five minutes to calm themselves, and catch their breaths before they could set the rest of Donato's plan into action.

Ghiberti had chosen his hiding place well; the cave was limestone, and it made any type of digging impossible. During high tide the water pressure against the door would force it shut, so the only time that the cave could be accessed was in the morning when the tide was low. His final safeguard was the special magnetic key that Leonardo had designed to thrust a series of pulleys and levers. These were needed to move the great weight of the limestone door open or closed. Ghiberti had used Leonardo's magnetic key to bolt the entrance. He knew there was no other key like it in the world. What Ghiberti did not know was that Leonardo had made a wax mold of the key, and that he had given a copy of it to Bischero who was on his way.

Meanwhile, Donato was preparing Pasquale and Bischero for the plan of attack.

"I am surprised to see that Ghiberti does not have any guards posted. Ghiberti is too smart to leave his fortress unprotected, so we will have to keep a sharp lookout. I have my men positioned at the northern and southern points, but that leaves us vulnerable at the cave's entrance. Mimmo and I will go first. When we give the signal, you two can swim across. If you see or hear the slightest sound or movement, signal us with a wave," advised Donato. He was tense.

He knew that he had to be prepared for anything. His instincts were telling him that the calm was a trap waiting to be sprung. Donato felt confident, since his men were well trained, and well positioned. He had done all that he could up to this point; now it was time to execute his plan. Silently, Mimmo, and Donato swam smoothly and quietly through the water with their heads cresting just at the surface. In a swift and synchronized motion, they pulled themselves up and onto the shore's edge.
The silence seemed to press in around them as an unseen force. While they waited, moments seemed like hours to Pasquale and Bischero. Finally, Donato gave them the signal to swim across.
Pasquale and Bischero slunk forward from the shadows. Slowly and cautiously they swam. Bischero could hear his heart beating in his chest. He was worried that the pounding would break the silence and give their position away. As he swam closer to Donato and Mimmo, Bischero could see the slick reflection of water on the limestone platform.

It had been worn smooth from the river's water currents over the centuries. He was thinking how he had slipped in the wet fountain at the palace, and he did not want to repeat the experience. So, Bischero sucked-in his breath, and held on tightly as Donato lifted him out of the water.

Once their feet touched the surface of the stone, and they were on dry ground, Ghiberti's men attacked from every direction. Resembling specters, hidden in the darkness, they flew out of every crevice to the north and from the south. Donato's men were taken by surprise. Then, like a tsunami, a great wave of water rose from the Arno River and up jumped four of Ghiberti's men and attacked Donato and Mimmo on the platform. Pasquale pulled Bischero back up against the cave wall to safety. There was no place for them to run. All they could do was watch as the battle unfolded.

Donato and his small band were trapped. It was four against two. Donato knew their only chance would be to move the battle from the platform to the depths of the water. Bravely, he and Mimmo charged head long into Ghiberti's men and rammed them backwards into the river. Down they went, deep into the murky water. Bischero and Pasquale lost sight of them, and all that remained was a turbulence on the water's surface.

Below the water's surface, Donato and Mimmo wrestled with their opponents, and kept them submerged. Wrestling is a battle of strength, and a test of wills, and Donato was a champion. It was how he had gotten his name "The Magnificent". With great speed and agility they churned round and round in the water. The warriors gnawed and gnashed at each other with razor sharp teeth.

Any shrieks of pain were muffled, and absorbed into the Arno's depths. One at a time Ghiberti's men popped up, floating face first in the water. Then Donato exploded upwards in one smooth motion. Grasping a huge breath of air as he somersaulted in midair, he quickly dove head long back down into the battle below. Mimmo did the same. Meanwhile, Bischero and Pasquale squinted as they strained to watch the dark scene unfold beneath the murky waters.

Bischero admired the athletic skills of his friends as the battle raged on. When Ghiberti's men were finally defeated, Donato returned to the surface. Donato was not surprised to see his men waiting to receive him. They had all converged around the cave to ensure their leader's safety. Bischero had never seen so many nutrias gathered together at one time. He was surprised at their numbers. They were too many to count. Donato's men had won the day, and captured the rest of Ghiberti's men. The only one who was missing was Ghiberti himself!

Bischero wondered, where could he be? He knew he had to enter the cave and destroy Leonardo's invention, but who or what would he find inside the cave?

CHAPTER SEVEN
Ghiberti's Escape

Bischero (Bee ska row) removed the purple pouch from his pocket that held the magnetized coin. He then found the octagon shaped depression carved out in the rose-colored limestone and inserted it like a puzzle piece. Nothing happened. So he removed the coin and inserted it face down. In a matter of moments he could hear the tumblers roll into place as the magnetized bolt thrust across the great weight, and the cave door smoothly slid open.

Mimmo (Mee moe) went ahead of Bischero to make sure that it was safe to enter. When he first walked into the cave, he could see a reflection bouncing off some mirrors that had been strategically placed in the cavern walls.

Mimmo was able to see all Donato's men at the entrance who were standing on the limestone platform. The image cast against the stone spanned the entire side of the wall. It was as big as "The Primavera" and "The Birth of Venus" painted by Botticelli (Boat tee chell ee).

"Ghiberti (Ghee bear tee) is a genius," exclaimed Mimmo.

Donato (Doe not toe) was right behind Mimmo.

"No wonder there were not any guards posted outside. From this standpoint, Ghiberti and his men could see everything happening outside of the cave without being seen or heard. Very clever; be on the alert, Mimmo," said Donato. "Ghiberti could be watching us as we speak."

As the foursome entered, one by one, they were awed to see a phosphorous interior that illuminated the cave. Ghiberti had done an incredible job. He had made sure that the cave was equipped with everything a varmint would need to live each day in comfort, and for a long period of time. The cave was a palace.

The cavern was enormous. From the ceiling hung stalactites of various lengths and colors.

They looked like ice cream cones stuck to the ceiling with little drops of water that slowly dropped to the cave floor below. Ghiberti used the water drops as an indoor sprinkling system for his vegetable garden.

The garden was square with rows and rows of fresh green sprigs shooting upwards from the soil. Placed in every third row was a round terra cotta oven. These ovens kept the plants warm so they could grow big and tall. On either side of the garden stood two pyramid shaped statues with three turtles holding up the crown just like the ones in Piazza Santa Maria Novella. To the right of the garden was a covered patio that had four cypress trees in each corner. The roof was made with braided straw that formed into a lattice shape. Woven through the triangular openings of the straw lattice were grape vines. Luscious purple and golden green grapes dangled down in clusters. While passing under the patio, Donato, Mimmo, Bischero and Pasquale could not resist plucking a grape or two and popping them into their mouths. The taste was juicy sweet and delicious.

On the other side of the garden the cavern floor slanted upwards forming a slight hill. On top of the hill Ghiberti had constructed a Greek temple with four marble columns and Doric capitals. On the ground was a mound of straw piled high. This had to be Ghiberti's sleeping quarters. From here he had an overview of the whole cavern. Directly in front of the temple was a beautiful lake that flowed up against a stone wall waterfall. The stone was streaked with the colors of the rainbow, which appeared to pour into water. The colors shined as the water cascaded down the front of the waterfall and filled the lake. To the left of the lake was a light torch that illuminated a passageway that went deeper into the rose-colored limestone.

The passageway was narrow and it led to a locked door. The door was wooden and placed at its mid-section was a colorful glazed terra cotta plate like the ones made by Luca della Robbia in Piazza dell'Annunziata. In the center was another octagon shape. Once again, Bischero took out his coin and placed it into the empty space and the door opened forward on its own. Behind the door was yet another cavern, smaller than the main cavern, but nonetheless beautiful. There were some large stalactites that reached down to the floor which were joined in the middle to stalagmites. (These look like upside down ice cream cones that are attached to the ground.) Others had not quite joined together to form natural columns. The ceiling was covered with purple amethyst crystals, and there was a gentle wind that could be felt coming from above, but from "where" exactly was impossible to determine.

Along the wall's edge was a small white river formed out of Carrara marble. It came from under the great cave wall and vanished into another wall across the cavern. The water glistened from an underground light source that illuminated the amethyst crystals above.

In the center of the room was a table carved from a marble block. It was covered with all different shapes and sizes of charcoal colored rocks. At either end of the table stood a candle with its own reflecting mirror. In the middle of the table was a fruit bowl made of hand blown glass, like the kind that are made on the island of Murano. In the center of the fruit bowl was an unusual looking rock that sparkled with flakes of gold, and was streaked with dark lines of smooth, solid black.

Suspended from the ceiling hung cut mirrors and white crystals that looked like snowflakes. It was an awesome display of twinkling lights. This was the machine that Bischero had to destroy.

Pasquale was the first to break the silence, "Look at this, Bischero. How are we going to destroy a machine of this size?"

Bischero began to explain, "Leonardo placed an extra stone into the sequence that is not needed. It is all that prevents the machine from working. Leonardo calls it the 'key stone' because once it is removed it will open up the passage way of light that will turn those lead pieces on the table into gold. That is why Leonardo was so concerned. He knew that in order for his machine to work, all Ghiberti would have to do is take away one stone."

"How do you know which one is the key stone?" asked Pasquale.

Hidden behind a boulder, Ghiberti jumped out. With acid in his voice he demanded, "Yes, Bischero. Which one is it?"

Ghiberti snapped his razor sharp teeth at Bischero as a warning. The images of his three friends eating played through his mind, as he remembered them ripping the dead lizards limb from limb. The horror and nauseating sickness of those moments had been impressed into his mind forever. Bischero was really scared.

No one had ever wanted to hurt him before, and now Ghiberti was threatening to rip him apart like Bischero had seen his friends devour their breakfast.

He tried to think of something dear to him so that he would not be afraid. Miscia (Me sha), his sweet cat, was the only thing that popped into his mind. Who would love and care for his little Miscia if he were not around? The more he focused on Miscia, the more his heart started beating to a calmer rhythm: tick, tock, tick, tock, like the metronome. Bischero felt safe and a peace flooded over him. Then, BOOM! Bischero transformed into the image of his cat Miscia.

Everyone knows that a cat is a rat's mortal enemy, and a nutria is like a big rat, after all. The sight of Miscia paralyzed Ghiberti with fear, and he turned tail and ran for the small lake that was fed by the cavern waterfall. Ghiberti jumped into the center of the lake and disappeared.

CHAPTER EIGHT
Bischero Turns on the Invention

Donato (Doe not toe) sent two of his men in pursuit of Ghiberti (Ghee bear tee). After about five minutes his men returned through the front entrance of the cave. They reported to Donato that Ghiberti had escaped in the labyrinth of underwater tunnels that lay below the cavern. They had gotten lost and were relieved to find the air pocket outside the cave just in time.

Donato imagined that this is where Ghiberti's four men had come from when they surprised Mimmo (Mee moe) and himself at the platform. It would take Donato's men awhile before they would be able to uncover all the routes below, and to figure out where they led.

Ghiberti was very clever indeed, but now the fortress belonged to the D'Ambras. It was a giant victory for the Florentine nutrias. Ghiberti had been banished from their waters, and Donato hoped to never see the likes of him again. He sent word for his men to post lookouts from Florence to Pisa. If he did try to return, Donato was determined to not make it easy for him.

Donato returned to Bischero (Bee ska row) and Pasquale (Paw squal lay) in the inner cavern. He assured them that Ghiberti would not be returning anytime soon. Now the question was "what" to do with Leonardo's machine?

Bischero thoughtfully spoke. "Leonardo gave me instructions to destroy the machine in front of Ghiberti's eyes. If that was not possible, then Leonardo advised me to place his work under your protection, Donato. You are the only one with strength enough to keep it safe. It will be protected in several ways. First, it will be in this fortress under guard. Second, I'm the only one who knows which is the key stone and I will take it with me. What Ghiberti does not know is at which point the key stone is to be removed. If it is not done at the correct time, the whole machine will explode into a giant fire ball."

Bischero walked toward the cavern door. "Last, Leonardo taught me how to increase the strength of the magnets so that I will be the only one able to change and re-master the key."

56

Then he closed the door so only Donato and Pasquale were left inside with him. Once the door was sealed shut, Bischero lit the candles on either side of the table. The mirrors reflected light beams upwards into the suspended crystals. It was interesting to watch as the beams of light traveled from one crystal to another and against another mirror to send the beam of light into another direction. The cavern was extraordinarily brilliant with light.

Pasquale said, "Now what happens Bischero?"
"Well," said Bischero, "now we wait for the sun to rise in the right spot. Do you feel that draft of air, Pasquale?"

He and Donato both nodded their heads, yes.

"Leonardo explained to me that the sun has to shine downwards and touch all the mirrors and crystals from above. It is the combination of the two streams of light that will heat the lead to just the right temperature so that it will convert to gold. I am guessing that the only access for the sun to shine in here is through that small wind tunnel that we feel," explained Bischero.

"Now, when the sun starts to shine, you and Donato need to jump behind that boulder, the same one where Ghiberti had hid earlier," instructed Bischero.

As the sun began to shine through the wind tunnel, a glow filled the cavern. Donato and Pasquale were the first ones to jump behind the boulder, and Bischero followed a few moments later. He told them to cover their eyes until the light faded out.

57

The temperature of the cavern grew very hot, but the limestone walls absorbed much of the heat so it worked as a shield to protect the three compatriots.

They stayed behind the boulder for almost an hour, until the heat and light faded to a tolerable level. Bischero cracked opened his eyes just a little to see if it was safe to open them completely. When he was sure it was safe, he told Donato and Pasquale they could uncover their eyes. Slowly, they stood up and looked over the boulder to the center table. There, across the table, sparkled solid gold where there had once been only pieces of lead. Bischero was the first to speak.

"Now that we have all witnessed the change, we know just how dangerous this machine is, and that no one must be allowed to get near it. Since Ghiberti directed the light through a hole in the limestone mountain, this means that there will only ever be one time during the day that I will be able to change the lead into gold. This will make it safer for everyone," said Bischero.

Then he pulled out the key stone from his pocket and showed it to Donato and Pasquale.

Pasquale said, "That is the rock that was on the glass bowl in the center of the table. It is so strange looking. What kind of a rock is it?"

Bischero answered, "It is a rock that flew out of the heavens. One night Leonardo was sitting on a hilltop in Fiesole (Fee A so lay), and a great light streaked across the sky. As he watched, the light fell to earth and Leonardo chased after it until he found the place where it hit the ground. Leonardo says it is special, and that there is not another stone like it.

58

He calls it the Philosopher's Stone. It is what makes the light change to the right temperature, and transforms the lead into gold. Feel how heavy it is."

He handed it first to Pasquale and then to Donato. Donato picked up a large piece of gold in one hand, and weighed it against the Philosopher's Stone in the other. It was at least three times heavier.

Donato asked Bischero, "Why is gold so important?"

Bischero replied, "Leonardo told me that money is what runs the world of men, and that humans will do anything for gold. He says that the love of money is the root of all evil, and that Ghiberti would have been able to rule over man with this kind of power. Leonardo did not want to see anyone get hurt because of Ghiberti's greed for power and control.

Gold is money and it can buy food, textiles for clothes, and building materials for homes to shelter families. He also believes that gold can be used to make healing potions, and he is still working on this theory. He says that it is an ancient theory that goes back to the times of Aristotle and Plato, and it is the lost art of Alchemy."

Bischero thought of Leonardo waiting for him, and so Bischero took the Philosopher's Stone and placed it into his pocket.

"Come on Pasquale. We must get back to Leonardo and tell him all that has happened." Bischero shook hands with Donato and thanked him for his help. He and Pasquale ran back to the limestone platform and dove back into the Arno.

Bischero instantly shape-shifted into a salmon and raced Pasquale back to the shoreline of Leonardo's workshop.

When they neared the surface by the shore, Bischero propelled himself forward with a final thrust to reach the land. In a blink of an eye, he shape-shifted back into his natural form. Pasquale was right behind him, and with his mighty webbed feet, he gave a final launch, and beat Bischero to the landing by half a second.

Dripping wet, the two boys did not have much of a chance to catch their breaths because Leonardo stood in front of them–he had been anxiously waiting for their return. He wanted to know the outcome, and urged the boys to tell him everything that had happened. Bischero and Pasquale took turns telling him the whole story. It was the only way they could gather enough breath to get the story out.

Leonardo listened patiently until the two boys had gotten out every detail. Then Leonardo led them back into his workshop in silence. He was thinking.

"Bischero," Leonardo began. "I must leave for Milan this very night. You must stay here for a week or two and finish school. Once classes are finished for the summer, you must join me. Remember, you must keep the secret of turning lead into gold to yourself. Knowledge is power, and it would be dangerous to share what you know with anyone. You must promise to live a simple life, and you will never be without money for your travels or to help others in need.

I have thought about your special gifts as a druid too. I want you to understand that you must always keep these abilities a secret as well.

Just as the chameleon does not tell how he changes colors, your body can do things that others cannot, and people will be cruel to you if they discover that you are different. I know, because I do not think like other people, and I have been ridiculed, laughed at, and some have even accused my scientific discoveries as being mystical. What rubbish! What people do not understand, they are afraid of and their behavior can turn to violence.

I do not know why my brain works differently than others, nor do I know why most people can see colors and some cannot; they are color blind. I do not know why I can talk to animals, and others cannot. There are so many mysteries that God has left us with to figure out on our own. Life is a great puzzle. I believe not knowing everything is a gift. It allows us to question and search for answers. The search can take us on many wonderful adventures, and teach us many lessons in life.

Now, I have left you with some florins in the wall where the coin was hidden. When you have finished with school, you must join me in Milan. Talk with Donato and he will show you how to pay for passage on an outgoing boat. I have left instructions with him in case you need to reach me. Do not be worried, little Bischero. I will see you in about a month. Pasquale, you must accompany Bischero and watch over him in my absence. You boys did a fine job and I am really proud of you, but I must leave on the next ship north. Now skedaddle while I pack, and stay out of trouble."

Leonardo gave Bischero a tight hug that squeezed the air out of him. He gently stroked Pasquale on the head, and the boys ran out the door.

"Where do you want to go Bischero?" asked Pasquale.

"Let's go up to Michelangelo's favorite hill. I like to call it Piazzale Michelangelo. Michelangelo likes to go there when he thinks. He is the one who helped me make up my poem 'Contemplatin'." I ran up there one day when I was feeling sad and lonely. He found me sitting on a log watching the creatures in the forest. He asked me what I was contemplating. When I told him I did not know what that word meant, he just laughed. He told me it was just a big word for thinking big thoughts, like thinking about your destiny. You want to go there? Maybe Michelangelo is there," asked Bischero.

"Sure. Let's go!" answered Pasquale.

CHAPTER NINE
What Happened to Ghiberti?

When the boys reached the top of the hill, they found they were all alone. Sitting on the hilltop overlooking Florence was very serene. It was a perfect Florentine day. The sky was cobalt blue and there was not a cloud in sight. The beauty took the boys' breaths away.

Then Pasquale (Paw squal lay) turned to Bischero (Bee ska row) and asked, "What is Destiny? I hear people talking about it all the time."

Bischero squinched up his face in deep thought for a moment or two. Then he said, "I remember my papa talked about it with Leonardo once.

They agreed that it is a path which a person's life follows, and that he has little control over it. All he can do is learn to make good choices instead of bad ones, and that it is all in the divine hands of God."

Quietly, Bischero and Pasquale sat on the hilltop "contemplatin" their destines. Suddenly, out of nowhere, a ghastly explosion erupted that shook the trees, Va Va VA VOOM!!!!!!!

Bischero jumped to his feet. He shouted, "Pasquale, what was that?"

Sheepishly, Pasquale answered, "I broke wind."

Bischero replied, "Yah! You sure broke somethin'!"

Embarrassed, Pasquale tried to explain, "It must have been something I ate."

Stunned, Bischero said, "Imagine that."

Defensively, Pasquale continued, "It's not my fault. It's, it's, it's Destiny!"

Then, the two friends burst into laughter.

Through their tears of laughter Bischero and Pasquale could see Mimmo (Mee moe) charging up the hill toward them. Breathlessly, Mimmo struggled to get out his words. "Bischero! Pasquale! You must return to Palazzo D'Ambra! Word has traveled from Venice to The Magnificent. Ghiberti (Ghee bear tee) is in Venice, and the prince requests your presence.

The Magnificent has made arrangements for you to depart on a ship that is leaving port within the hour. Hurry, The Magnificent must speak with you before you leave!"

Bischero and Mimmo anxiously raced down the hill into another adventure. As for Pasquale, he tripped over his feet and tumbled all the way down the hill, and so begins another story.

It is said that Bischero can be spotted even to this day on the streets, or in the shops of Florence. He can disguise himself as a hungry child, or a silent old man. He especially likes to watch the children while they are in the toy shops and restaurants with their parents. If you look closely, you may even spot him. He watches to see who is behaving and who is not.

For those children who behave as they should, it is said that they will receive a fantastic adventure when they least expect it, and they will be rewarded with a special memento to cherish and remember always. That is how I got my necklace.

You see, he spotted me while I was buying a gelato ice cream for a lonely child that I did not know. He then shared his story with me so that I could pass it onto you. In the end, he handed me this necklace made of silver so that I would always remember how special it is to be a child, and how important it is to share God's love with everyone.

Ding, ding! Ding, ding! Oops, there goes the seat belt warning. Now you boys need to buckle-up so that we can safely land in Florence, but I'll be going on to Venice.

If you should happen to visit this city of wonder, you will be able to find me in Piazza San Marco. I will be at a little café, sipping on a cappuccino. I will be there each morning by eight o'clock, and I'll be happy to share another Bischero adventure. I'll tell you how he saved Venice from being destroyed by Ghiberti, and how he almost blew up the city.

ARTWORK
Where You Can Find It

"The Birth of Venus"
By Sandro Botticelli
Located in the Uffizi Museum in Florence,
Italy
2nd Floor, 10-14 Botticelli Room

"Primavera"
By Sandro Botticelli
Located in the Uffizi Museum in Florence,
Italy
2nd Floor, 10-14 Botticelli Room

"The Annunciation"
By Leonardo da Vinci
Located in the Uffizi Museum in
Florence, Italy
2nd Floor, 15 Leonardo Room

"The Vitruvian Man"
By Leonardo da Vinci
Located in the Gallerie dell'Accademia in Venice,
Italy
You must ask if it is on display to the public.
It is fragile, and not always on view.

"Self Portrait"
By Leonardo da Vinci
Located in the Uffizi Museum in Florence, Italy

....

"The Magnificent"
By Vasari
Located in the Uffizi Museum in Florence, Italy

....

"Savonarola"
By Fra Bartolomeo
Located in the Monastery in Piazza San Marco in
Florence, Italy

....

"Savonarola Burned at the Stake"
By Unknown Artist
Located in the Monastery in Piazza San
Marco in Florence, Italy

....

"Medici Coin"
By Unknown Artist
Located in the Uffizi Museum in Florence, Italy

☐

"David"
A reproduction of Michelangelo's David
Located at Piazzale Michelangelo, in Florence, Italy

☐

AUTHOR'S TRIVIA

The Introduction is a true story, it really happened, and it explains the circumstances which allowed the story to pop into my head. The only changes I made were, that the Bischero pendant was really Pinocchio, that there were actually two little girls, and I changed them to boys, whom I named after my sons, Joshua and Zachari. Of course, I am/was the lady mentioned in the intro. The introduction is brief, and is my vehicle to transport the reader from the present to the past. I hope you liked it.

In CHAPTER ONE, the reader learns that Bischero has blond hair, and soft brown eyes that sparkle with a touch of gold and green that warm a body's heart just to look at them; these describe my son Zachari. The reader also learns that Bischero's birthday is December 15th. In fact, this is the birthday of my son Joshua. Giuseppe is also introduced, and this is the name of my father. It is a tribute to my dad, whom I loved very much, but sadly, he is no longer in this world.

Further along in CHAPTER ONE, the reader learns that Miscia the cat has allergies, and sinus problems. Miscia was a real cat who lived with me in Florence, Italy during the time I was studying at the university, and just like the cat in my story, she had terrible allergies and gross sinus problems.

In CHAPTER TWO, the reader learns a poem, "Contemplatin". I actually wrote this while I was sitting on a bench in the little forest that grows between the city of Florence and Piazzale Michelangelo. The poem describes what I was seeing in front of me, and how it made me feel. In my mind's eye, the surroundings brought me back home because the area reminded me of a Huck Finn adventure by Mark Twain.

Finally, each of my characters throughout the remainder of the story take on attributes of people I know, or have human historical counterparts. These characters give you a window into my world of imagination, and I hope you enjoy them as much as I do.

What inspired me to create this series? I studied in Florence for over three years, and it was during this time that many people would ask me the same questions. "What is there to see while I am in Florence?" My response was, "How long do you plan to be in the city?" I learned that the average stay in Florence was one to three days. Most often, people were traveling in tour groups, and only had a day to sightsee. Then, I learned that these same folks all had similar complaints. "One city blurs into the next. After a while, every church looks like the last. There is nothing for our children to do. Every museum seems like all the rest. How do you distinguish them apart?" I thought, "I" could solve all of these problems in a story. With my airplane experience in hand, I put it all together, and so it began.

71

CROSS WORD PUZZLE

Bischero in Florence

www.CrosswordWeaver.com

ACROSS

1 Who is Bischero's enemy?
4 What is the name of Bishero's adopted father?
8 What is the name of the greatest mind of all time?
9 What is the name of the river where the king of the nutria lives?

DOWN

2 Who is the king of the Nutria?
3 What is the name of Bischero's cat"
4 How do you say "Thank You" in Italian?
5 Who is Bischero's best friend, who is an animal?
6 What is Ghiberti trying to create?
7 What was the name of the city where Bischero lived?

CROSS WORD PUZZLE SOLUTION

Bischero in Florence

Solution:

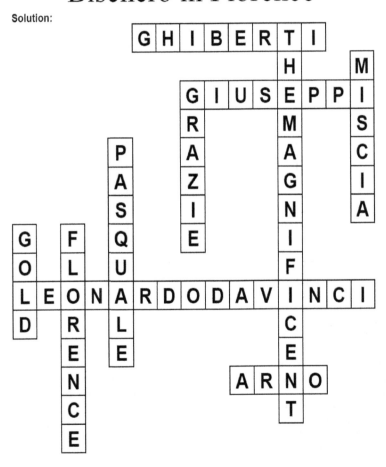

COLOR ME PAGES

Bischero wakes up to meet Giuseppi and Miscia for the first time.

Pasquale and Bischero meet for the first time on the shoreline.

Leonardo da Vinci, Bischero, and Pasquale looking at the "Vitruvian Man" in Leonardo's workshop.

Donato standing in front of the statue of Gianna, as Bischero watches, and hides in the distance.

Bischero standing on the mound of Amfwyn in a dream.

**Donato "The Magnificent" and Mimmo, his first
in command, battle against Ghiberti's men in the
Arno River.**

Ghiberti comes out from hiding in the cave, and is ready to attack.

Bischero turns lead into gold and shows the keystone to Donato and Pasquale.

Pasquale and Bischero at Piazzale Michelangelo; laughing because Pasquale just broke wind.